Before using these books...

☞ A teacher/counselor manual is separately available for guiding students in the use of these workbooks.

✎ To prevent bleed-through, it is recommended that water-based, rather than spirit-based, markers or pens be used in this workbook.

Important

This book is not intended as a treatment tool or to be utilized for diagnostic or investigative purposes. It is not designed for and should not be recommended or suggested for use in any unsupervised, self-help or self-therapy setting, group or situation. Professionals who use this book are exercising their own professional judgement and take full responsibility for doing so.

The STARS LifeSkills Program

Teacher/Counselor Manual

Learning About Anger

Learning More About Anger

Knowing Yourself

Getting Along with Others

Respecting Others

How Drugs and Alcohol Affect Us

How Drugs and Alcohol Affect Us

Jan Stewart
Illustrated by Cecilia Bowman
ISBN 978-1-63026-833-6

© 2003 Jan Stewart and Hunter House
Design and layout Jinni Fontana © 2003 Hunter House
First U.S. edition published in 2003 by Hunter House.

For further information, contact Hunter House, Inc.

STARS: Steps to Achieving Real-life Skills

How Drugs and Alcohol Affect Us

Dear Student:

This workbook is part of a program to help you learn some real-life skills. You may already have some of these skills, and the information may just be a reminder or a review. If the information is new to you, then it is possible for you to learn skills and strategies that can help you for the rest of your life.

If you are unable to complete any section, leave it blank and come back to it later. If you are still unsure, ask your parent or guardian to assist you. If this is not possible, ask the person who gave you the workbook. On the next page there is a glossary of words that are used in the workbook. Read this before you begin.

Please remember to have your parent or guardian fill out the last page.

Thank you for your cooperation.

Name of Student: _____

Adviser: _____

Assignment Date: _____

Completion Date: _____

Glossary

Addiction—inability to give something up such as drugs, alcohol or gambling

Anxiety—feeling of tension or nervousness

Balance—feeling of stability or steadiness

Chronic—something that goes on for a long time

Concentration—focusing your attention

Confidence—being sure of yourself

Conviction—found guilty

Deny—say you didn't do something or that it isn't true

Depression—feeling of extreme sadness and inadequacy

Dilemma—a difficult problem to decide about

Distort—twist out of shape, not see something clearly

Encourage—cheer up or assist another person by supporting them

Habit—something done regularly

Illegal—against the law

Imply—hint at something or suggest something

Intoxicated—drunk or out of control

Irritable—grouchy or easily angered

Judgment—good sense, an opinion

Long-term—lasting a long time

Memory—a person's store of mental information

Motivation—reason for doing something

Sensitive—quite easily affected by something external

Short-term—lasting for a short time

Visualize—picture something in your mind

How Drugs and Alcohol Affect Us

A drug is any substance taken to change a person's physical, mental, or emotional state. Some drugs are legal and others are illegal. Some drugs are harmful and others are helpful. When drugs are taken for medical reasons, they are helpful. Some drugs aren't taken for medical reasons; rather, they're taken to alter the way the brain functions or to experience a "high." These drugs can have very harmful effects on the user. Drugs may also be harmful when they are not prescribed, too much is taken, or they are taken along with other drugs which combine with them in a bad way.

- Nicotine is a drug.

- Alcohol is a drug.

This unit includes information about the following topics:

- Drug Facts

- Why People Use Drugs

- Drug Advertising

- The Path from Use to Abuse

- Excuses and Defenses

- Risks of Drug Use

- Setting Goals

- Solving Problems and Making Wise Decisions

Some of the information in this unit will not directly relate to you. However, learning more about any topic is always helpful. It may be useful to you in the future if you are faced with making a decision. Making an informed decision is always better than making a decision without information. With the information you learn, you may also be able to help someone you know.

If you do use drugs, no one but you can make you stop. If you aren't ready now, you may be ready in the future. Working on this unit may give you some valuable information about where you may be headed with your drug use. Counselors, teachers, parents, and friends can help you when you are ready to stop using drugs.

What Do You Already Know About Drugs and Alcohol?

Using the space below, write a list of the facts that you already know about drugs and alcohol. Write another list of things about drugs and alcohol that you would like to know more about.

What I know... _____

_____

_____

_____

_____

_____

What I want to know more about... _____

_____

_____

_____

_____

_____

Test Your Knowledge

Take the following mini-quiz about drugs and alcohol. **Check either True or False.**

1. A drug can cause short-term confusion.

    ☐ True   ☐ False

2. A drug is a substance that when taken into the body can change the way a body functions.

    ☐ True   ☐ False

3. Drugs cause only short-term effects and they wear off over time.

    ☐ True   ☐ False

4. Most drug users are from disadvantaged families.

    ☐ True   ☐ False

5. A depressant makes your body speed up.

    ☐ True   ☐ False

6. Alcohol is a stimulant.

    ☐ True   ☐ False

7. Drinking "hard liquor" is worse for you than just drinking beer.

    ☐ True   ☐ False

8. Someone's weight will influence their blood-alcohol level.

☐ True   ☐ False

9. Coffee will help you sober up.

☐ True   ☐ False

10. Alcohol contributes to approximately 70% of murders and violent crimes.

☐ True   ☐ False

11. Long-term use of alcohol can lead to muscle weakness.

☐ True   ☐ False

12. If a pregnant woman drinks alcohol, it will be directly carried to her unborn baby.

☐ True   ☐ False

13. Alcohol and marijuana are the most widely used drugs.

☐ True   ☐ False

14. A fatal alcohol-related car crash occurs about every 20 minutes in the United States.

☐ True   ☐ False

15. Drinking helps keep you warm when it is cold outside.

☐ True   ☐ False

Answers: 1. True; **2.** True; **3.** False: There are both long-term and short-term effects of drug use; **4.** False: Drug users come from all walks of life; **5.** False: Depressants slow down the body while stimulants speed up body functions; **6.** False: Alcohol is a depressant; **7.** False: A bottle of beer contains the same volume of alcohol as a standard glass of wine and a standard glass of hard liquor; **8.** True; **9.** False: Coffee may make you more alert, but it does not help get rid of alcohol in the body. Only time will help make someone sober again; **10.** True; **11.** True; **12.** True; **13.** False: Alcohol and tobacco are the most widely used drugs; **14.** True; **15.** False: Alcohol makes you lose more heat and therefore decreases your body temperature.

The STARS LifeSkills Program ★ How Drugs and Alcohol Affect Us   ©2003 Jan Stewart and Hunter House, Inc.

Choosing Drugs: Your Opinion

Why do you think people choose to use drugs? **List three reasons below.**

1. _____

2. _____

3. _____

Why do you think some people choose *not* to use drugs? **List three reasons below.**

1. _____

2. _____

3. _____

How would you describe the typical drug user?

_____

_____

Have you ever had to make an important decision or choice about something that could seriously affect your life? How did you feel about the results of that decision?

_____

_____

_____

What did you gain from making this decision?

_____

What did you lose from making this decision?

_____

Why Do People Use Drugs?

Different people use drugs for different reasons. People may start using drugs for one reason and then continue for another reason. The following are some common reasons people give for using drugs:

☐ To experiment (see what it is like)

☐ To have fun

☐ To get more courage

☐ To liven up a party

☐ To relax

☐ To forget about problems

☐ To rebel against authority

☐ To cope better

☐ To relieve stress

☐ To forget

☐ To satisfy curiosity

☐ To help get rid of emotions like anger, hurt, jealousy, anxiety, and depression

☐ To help get rid of boredom

☐ To gain more confidence

☐ To fit in

☐ To belong

☐ To get through the day

Take another look at the list above and put a check in the box next to the comments that you hear most often. Circle any reason you have used to justify drinking or using drugs. Write down the one main reason you would give for starting drinking or using drugs.

_____

Using the reason above, what are the disadvantages of using this excuse or reasoning?

_____

_____

_____

_____

The STARS LifeSkills Program ★ How Drugs and Alcohol Affect Us   ©2003 Jan Stewart and Hunter House, Inc.

Paying Attention to Ads

Some people find it more difficult not to use nicotine and alcohol because they are often given false promises regarding how using a product will make someone more attractive, popular, etc. These advertisement do not offer the "true story" about the effects of cigarettes and alcohol. Look at several ads for cigarettes or alcohol in magazines. **Choose one ad which features people and the product name in the ad.**

Describe how the people look in the ad. _____

_____

_____

_____

What does the product look like? **Pick three words to describe it.**

1. _____

2. _____

3. _____

How does this ad encourage people to use drugs? _____

_____

_____

What age group do you think the ad is for? _____

Write one sentence to describe what you think the advertisers want you to believe about their product.

_____

_____

The ad was taken from (magazine) _____ Issue: _____

Create Your Own Ad

Using the information in this unit, write your own ad to show the harmful effects of alcohol or cigarettes. You will want to advertise the benefits of not using drugs and living a healthy life. You may wish to do this activity once you have worked through the booklet so that you have more information to include in your ad.

The Path From Drug Use to Drug Abuse

Many people who work with drug and alcohol users state that the path from being a user to being an abuser has progressive stages. For some people the stages may occur quickly and for others they may take more time. Many factors affect how an individual will move through the stages, such as: how available the drugs and alcohol are, peer pressure or support, the person's personality, and the person's home life.

STAGE 1: Non-use

A person chooses not to use any drugs or alcohol. Some reasons people choose to not use drugs or alcohol are to maintain good health or because they have a medical condition such as diabetes. People may also choose not to use drugs or alcohol because of their family values or for religious reasons. People who are recovering from an alcohol or drug addiction are not able to use alcohol or drugs without it having serious effects on their lives. People recovering from an addiction have chosen a non-using lifestyle.

Do you know anyone who has chosen never to use drugs or alcohol?_____

Why do you think they made that choice?

_____

_____

_____

_____

_____

_____

_____

STAGE 2: Irregular Use

At this stage the user may try a substance once or several times. This is called experimenting. People may also use on an infrequent basis such as on special occasions. There is no specific pattern of use. If use continues after a few times, the person is choosing to move out of the experimentation phase and into a stage called irregular use. People may use drugs and alcohol in Stage 2 because they are curious, they would like to belong to a group, or they would like to be accepted by their peers.

Do you know anyone who is an irregular user of drugs or alcohol? _____

What are the clues that someone is in this stage?

_____

_____

_____

_____

_____

_____

_____

The STARS LifeSkills Program ★ How Drugs and Alcohol Affect Us   ©2003 Jan Stewart and Hunter House, Inc.

STAGE 3: Regular Use

Regular use means that there is a pattern of either frequent or infrequent use. An example of this is when people use drugs or alcohol once every month or at parties or on weekends. What separates Stage 3 from Stage 4 is that there is less harm to the user at Stage 3. The regular user takes drugs or drinks alcohol to experience the effects and using drugs or alcohol has become a part of his or her lifestyle.

Do you know anyone who is a regular user of drugs or alcohol? _____

What are the clues that someone is in this stage?

_____

_____

_____

_____

_____

_____

STAGE 4: Harmful Use

This stage could occur whether a person uses drugs or alcohol irregularly or regularly. **Once drug or alcohol use starts to affect one's life in any way, it is considered harmful.** Drug and alcohol use may result in harm when it interferes with the person's physical or mental health. When drug or alcohol use affects your relationships with friends or family, it is harmful. When drug or alcohol use decreases your functioning at work, home, or school, it is harmful. A person may be in the harmful stage even if his or her behavior has the potential for harm, such as when a person drinks and then drives. Even if he or she does not have an accident, the potential for harm is there and this is very dangerous. People sometimes reach this stage because they like to experience the feeling of taking drugs or drinking alcohol and they do not recognize the negative effects. People sometimes rely on their defenses to make this stage easier. You will learn more about this later.

Do you know anyone who is in the harmful use stage of using drugs or alcohol? _____

What are the clues that someone is in this stage?

_____

_____

_____

_____

_____

_____

The STARS LifeSkills Program ★ How Drugs and Alcohol Affect Us   ©2003 Jan Stewart and Hunter House, Inc.

STAGE 5: Dependent Use

At this stage, the person has come to rely on the drugs even though they result in serious harm. Some people may feel the need to use drug or alcohol to cope with problems, or to feel comfortable with other people. They may not use every day, but they're beginning to make drugs or alcohol the most important thing in their lives. These people put a lot of time and energy into planning to use drugs or alcohol, finding drugs or alcohol, and using drugs or alcohol. For some people, dependency can result in physical addiction. Physical addiction means that the person doesn't feel well unless he or she uses drugs or alcohol. Usually a person at the dependent stage needs help to recover. At this stage, many people use drugs or alcohol to feel "normal," or to avoid feeling sick or uncomfortable. Sometimes the user must take a larger amount of the drug or drink more because his or her body gets used to taking the drug; this is called building up a *tolerance*. They may feel like they have lost control of their drug or alcohol use. Many people make unsuccessful attempts to quit using, or to cut down the amount of drugs or alcohol they use. At this stage, users spend a lot of time recovering from the effects of using drugs or alcohol. Once they're dependent, they may not go back to using drugs like they did in the earlier stages. They must only go to stage one—which is non-use.

You will learn more later about how to help someone who is abusing drugs or alcohol.

Helping Others

Imagine that you had one friend in each of the stages from drug use to drug abuse. What would you say to your friend at each stage to help him or her? For instance, what could you do to warn them about the effects of using the drugs? What could stop them from going further down the path, or worse, getting to the end of the path?

STAGE 1: Non-use

_____

_____

STAGE 2: Irregular Use

_____

_____

STAGE 3: Regular Use

_____

_____

STAGE 4: Regular Use

_____

_____

STAGE 5: Dependent Use

_____

_____

The STARS LifeSkills Program ★ How Drugs and Alcohol Affect Us

Excuses and Defenses

People often protect themselves from unpleasant thoughts, feelings, and situations by using defenses. We may use defenses for many reasons: to ignore something; to make something appear like it isn't important; to change the truth; to make excuses for our behavior; or to make something appear like it's someone else's problem, and not our own. Defenses can keep you from facing the real situation. Using defenses may make the problem worse. The following are definitions and examples of four kinds of defenses.

Rationalizing

Making up excuses so that you can make something unacceptable appear acceptable.

Marni really likes a boy who's going to be at the same party as her on Saturday. She's very nervous about talking to him. Marni's friend Kathleen told her that she should smoke a joint before the party so that she can loosen up and talk to the boy. Marni decides that smoking a joint would help her relax, so she smokes before the party. **Marni made the excuse that she needed to smoke marijuana in order to calm herself. She rationalized using drugs.**

What are three things you have said yourself, or have heard friends or others say, to rationalize or make excuses for using drugs?

1._____

_____

2._____

_____

3._____

_____

Minimizing

Making something appear less serious or important than it is.

Eric had a party at his house on the weekend that his parents were away. His friend Graham came over and started drinking heavily. As the evening progressed, Graham became very intoxicated. He became argumentative and even violent and ended up breaking a chair, putting a large hole in the wall, and throwing up in the living room. The next day Graham said to Eric, "I wasn't that drunk and anyway, that's what happens when you have parties." Graham didn't apologize for his behavior. **Graham minimized the situation. The situation was very serious, and Graham made it seem like it was something unimportant.**

How might Eric solve this problem? What might he want to say to Graham in the future?

_____

_____

_____

_____

Denying

Not accepting reality.

Alberto sneaks out of school during every break and lunch hour to have a cigarette. He smokes between 12–15 cigarettes a day. When Alberto cannot have a cigarette, he becomes irritable and anxious. Alberto tells his friends that he is not addicted to cigarettes and he believes that if he wanted to, he could quit without a problem. **Alberto is denying that he is addicted to a drug.**

What are three things that someone might say when they are denying their drug use?

1. _____

_____

2. _____

_____

3. _____

_____

Blaming

Making other people, places, or things responsible for your behavior.

Anna was caught with a bottle of alcohol in her locker at school. The teacher who saw the alcohol sent Anna to the office. When Anna got to the office she screamed at the principal, "It's that stupid teacher's fault. She's the one with nothing better to do than walk around the school trying to pick on every kid she sees." **Anna is blaming her problem on the teacher.**

Imagine you were caught with drugs by one of your parents. Instead of using blaming as a defense, what two things could you say to your mom or dad to accept responsibility for having drugs?

1. _____

_____

2. _____

_____

18

The STARS LifeSkills Program ★ How Drugs and Alcohol Affect Us   ©2003 Jan Stewart and Hunter House, Inc.

How Well Do You Spot Defenses?

In the following example, underline the defenses that Ike uses and write the name of the defense on the line below the section.

Ike didn't have any money and he wanted to go out, so he convinced himself that it would be all right to take a little money out of his mom's purse because she had just gotten paid. He didn't think she would notice. Ike said to himself, "I'm only going to take a bit anyway, so it really isn't that bad."

_____

Ike went out and bought some marijuana from one of his friends at the mall. Ike smoked the joint and walked around the mall with some people who he kind of knew from school. After a while, Ike was hungry so he went into a store and stole some chips, a drink, and the latest Hot Rod magazine. The cashier caught him and called his parents to pick him up. When Ike's parents came he said to them, "It's no big deal, I only took some chips. Its not like I stole a car or anything."

_____

His dad noticed his red eyes and asked him what he'd been smoking. Ike responded, "I never smoked anything. I don't even know what drugs look like."

_____

He then rudely said to his dad, "This is your problem. If you would have just let me get a job, this never would have happened."

_____

This is an example of a person using defenses that are very harmful.

The Dangerous Side of Using Drugs

There are some significant risks of drug abuse. Many drugs have very undesirable side effects that can be potentially life-threatening.

Drugs can reduce your coordination, distort your senses, and impair your judgment. This can lead to serious **Safety Hazards.**

Drugs affect your **Physical Health.** Smoking can cause lung damage, alcohol use can lead to liver damage, "huffing" or sniffing can damage your nose and brain, and injecting drugs can lead to fatal infections.

Some drugs can lead to severe **Mental Health** risks. Drug abuse can result in personality disturbances, learning problems, and loss of memory.

Many drug users become **Physically Dependent** on the drug. These people suffer from "symptoms of withdrawal" when they no longer take the drug.

When someone finds it extremely difficult to stop thinking about using drugs and when their emotions and behaviors are influenced by the drug, the person is said to be **Psychologically Dependent.**

When a user needs increased amounts of the drug that means that he has built up a **Tolerance** to the drug. Over time the user will need to increase the amount that she takes and this can easily lead to an overdose. Some people also move to a different drug that has a stronger effect.

Sometimes users take an **Overdose** of a drug. This may be accidental because it is often difficult to know the potency of street drugs or exactly what goes into them. An overdose can lead to both physical and mental damage or even death.

Mixing Drugs is extremely dangerous and can cause very undesirable side effects. With street drugs you can never really be sure of what you are taking.

Using and possessing drugs is illegal and this can result in **Legal Action** such as a fine, imprisonment, and/or a criminal record.

Many **accidents, road injuries,** and **fatalities** are cause by drivers who are under the influence of alcohol or another kind of drug.

The STARS LifeSkills Program ★ How Drugs and Alcohol Affect Us   ©2003 Jan Stewart and Hunter House, Inc.

Using the information from the previous page, answer the following questions.

1. Drugs can _____ physical coordination, _____ the senses, or impair judgment.

2. Many _____ and deaths are caused by intoxicated people.

3. Smoking marijuana and tobacco can cause _____ damage.

4. When the drug user becomes used to a drug and can only function normally when using the drug, it means the person has a physical _____.

5. _____ dependence is when the drug is the focus of a person's thoughts, emotions, and activities.

6. When a user needs more and more of a drug to get the same effect, they have built up a _____ to that drug.

7. An overdose of any drug can cause _____.

8. You can never know what you are taking in _____.

9. A conviction for illegal possession of a drug can result in _____.

10. Drugs can become much more dangerous when they are _____.

The Long-Term and Short-Term Effects of Using Drugs and Alcohol

People use drugs and alcohol for the effects they have. Many of these effects are harmful. Some of them last only a short while (short-term) and some last for a long time or are permanent (long-term). **For the two groups of effects below, indicate whether they are long-term (L), or short-term (S).**

Effects of marijuana

_____ loss of motivation

_____ concentration and short-term memory impaired

_____ sense of space and time distorted

_____ respiratory damage

_____ anxiety

_____ depression

_____ red eyes

_____ dry mouth and throat

_____ types of cancer

Effects of alcohol

_____ dizziness

_____ slurred speech

_____ brain damage

_____ heart disease

_____ ulcers

_____ shakiness

_____ double vision

_____ types of cancer

_____ disruption of family, social and working life

The STARS LifeSkills Program ★ How Drugs and Alcohol Affect Us · ©2003 Jan Stewart and Hunter House, Inc.

Goal Setting

When we set goals for ourselves and we work toward something important to us, we are less likely to become sidetracked by negative influences like drugs, cigarettes, and alcohol. Sometimes the goal may take a long time to accomplish, and sometimes it may take a short time. Goals are referred to as either long-term goals or short-term goals. Goals may be related to school, careers, home projects, sports, hobbies, or even physical appearance.

What is a goal that you might have that would be related to school?

_____

_____

_____

Now break your large goal into short term and long term goals.

_____

_____

_____

What do you plan to do in the present? (These are your short-term goals.)

1. _____

2. _____

3. _____

What do you plan to do in the future? (These are your long-term goals.)

1. _____

2. _____

3. _____

Many goals can be broken down into even smaller goals. If your goal is to quit smoking in three months, you can break this up into smaller parts. For example, you can say that you will go from smoking 20 cigarettes a day to smoking only 15. After the next week, you may say that you will only smoke 10 cigarettes a day. The next month you may lower it to only five a day. You could continue to break this up into smaller parts so that you can celebrate some success along the way. Giving yourself a reward for success is also a great idea. If your goal was to be able to run for 30 minutes a day, what could your smaller goals be?

1. _____

2. _____

3. _____

Drawing Your Goals

Start with a picture of your final goal.

Now draw snapshots of your steps leading up to your final goal.

Step 1

Step 2

Step 3

Step 4

Rewards

Some people say that if they achieve their goals then they will go out to a movie or buy themselves a CD. People have their own ways to reward themselves. Sometimes, just taking a break is a reward. What would be some reasonable rewards you could give yourself when you accomplish a goal?

In the space below, draw your rewards.

©2003 Jan Stewart and Hunter House, Inc.

The STARS LifeSkills Program ★ How Drugs and Alcohol Affect Us

Making the Best Decisions about Drugs and Alcohol

You may need to make several decisions throughout your life related to drugs and alcohol. Everyone has a choice whether or not they will use drugs and alcohol. The difficult part is making the right decision at the right time. Making informed decisions is a skill that can be practiced and improved over time.

To help guide you through the process, remember the word **SOLVE.** This is what it stands for:

S   **State** the problem

O   **Outline** your options

L   **List** the good and bad points of the options you like

V   **Visualize** the outcome

E   **Execute** your plan and **evaluate** your results

State the problem. When you have a decision to make, state what the problem is and try to be as specific as possible. For example, suppose you were accused of stealing something in a store. You didn't steal anything, and you need to respond to the clerk without the situation getting out of control.

Outline your options. Decide what you can do about the situation. Brainstorm all the ideas you can think of. For example, in private you could approach the person accusing you and explain the situation; or you could call your parents to explain things to them. Think of all the ideas you can, and, if it's possible, write them down.

List the good and bad points of the options you like. Pick the options that you think are the best. Maybe some of your options could be changed or joined together into an even better idea. At this time you do not have to be worried about details.

Visualize the outcome. Go over some of your responses to the problem situation. Think to yourself: "What will happen if I…?" Think ahead and try to picture what the result will be if you choose a particular option. "How will it affect what I feel, need, and want? How will it affect others? How will it relate to what I and my family believe?" Once you have thought about the outcome of using your options, pick the best one and decide what you will do.

Execute your plan and evaluate your results. The final steps are to act out your plan and then see if you made a decision that helped you or not. Ask yourself, "Did things turn out the way I thought? Is the solution better than if I hadn't done anything? What are the consequences of this solution?" Remember, just like athletes need to practice their sport over and over again, you may need some practice to find the best solution to solve the problem. However, with a lot of practice, you can be a good decision maker!

Try using the SOLVE method to solve any of the following problems. **Choose one of the following problem situations and circle the number beside it.**

1. A friend has invited you to a party where you know there will be alcohol available.

2. You are standing with a group of three friends who are all passing around a cigarette and they want you to share it.

3. A person at school offers to give you a free sample of drugs.

4. A friend of yours is extremely sick because she has taken some drugs. She tells you not to tell anyone, but you are concerned because she is getting worse.

After you have chosen one situation, follow the SOLVE steps to work through the problem. You may need to use your imagination to decide on the entire situation.

S _____

_____

O _____

_____

L _____

_____

V _____

_____

E _____

Which part was the most difficult to do? _____

Explain why it was difficult. _____

_____

_____

The STARS LifeSkills Program ★ How Drugs and Alcohol Affect Us   ©2003 Jan Stewart and Hunter House, Inc.

How to Help

A user who recognizes and admits that he or she has a problem is already on the way to getting better. If the person isn't ready to work at not being a drug user, he or she may need to wait for a better time. For some people, living without drugs is very difficult. But sooner or later, they will want to live a healthy lifestyle.

If you or someone you know decided to try to stop using drugs, what could you or others do to help them?

What would or could get in the way of achieving the goal?

Example

1. Support from home

2. Alternative activities such as a job or sports

Example

1. Not willing to change

2. Very few non-using friends

List two more:

1. _____

2. _____

List two more:

1. _____

2. _____

Imagine that your best friend were caught up with using drugs. You have noticed some very serious changes in him or her (for example, your friend has lost friends, is often sick, has stolen money to buy more drugs, and is not doing as well in school). You want to help and you have decided to write a letter of advice. What could you write that might encourage your friend to stop using drugs? **Write your letter on the next page.**

Write a letter of advice below to encourage your friend to stop using drugs.

Dear _____.

_____

_____

_____

_____

_____

_____

_____

_____

_____

_____

_____

_____

_____

Your Friend _____

The STARS LifeSkills Program ★ How Drugs and Alcohol Affect Us   ©2003 Jan Stewart and Hunter House, Inc.

Who to Turn to for Help

There are many organizations that help adults and young people who have concerns about alcohol and other drugs. They also help people who already have an addiction.

Write the name and phone numbers of three of these organizations in your community below:

1. _____ telephone number: _____

2. _____ telephone number: _____

3. _____ telephone number: _____

There are many individuals who can also help you or a friend by providing support, advice and referrals. These individuals may include teachers, parents, counselors, coaches, doctors, friends, ministers, rabbis, other religious or church leaders, and personnel from other special groups, associations, or organizations.

List three individuals you could turn to for help, or to get help for a friend:

1. _____ telephone number: _____

2. _____ telephone number: _____

3. _____ telephone number: _____

The most important thing to remember about drug and alcohol use is to get help immediately. The path of drug and alcohol use is destructive, and without support it can be very harmful. Learning to recognize a problem and then working to solve it takes a lot of strength and courage.

Journal Writing–Reflecting

Take a moment to think about the work you have done in this workbook. **Jot down some words about how you felt working on this workbook.** From there, use a sentence starter to write about what you have accomplished. Pick the sentence starter that you like and write a paragraph about anything you want. This is a chance for you to be creative and to write something for yourself. Use the space below and a separate sheet if necessary.

If you are better with pictures, feel free to draw a picture.

Sentence Starters

From the information in this workbook, I learned…

I have never really thought about…

In the future, …

Thinking back now, I wish that I would have…

_____

_____

_____

_____

_____

_____

_____

_____

The STARS LifeSkills Program ★ How Drugs and Alcohol Affect Us   ©2003 Jan Stewart and Hunter House, Inc.

How Drugs and Alcohol Affect Us

Parents/Guardians

It would be helpful if you could review and comment on the work that your child has done in this workbook. We encourage students to work with their parents on certain sections and we thank you for your cooperation. We hope that your child has had a chance to examine their behavior and to plan positively for the future. This unit has exposed students to a lot of information which we hope could be reviewed at home. We greatly appreciate your partnership in this project.

Comments: _____

_____

_____

_____

_____

_____

_____

Please feel free to contact the student's advisor or the person who assigned this workbook if you have any other questions or concerns.

Students

Now that you have completed the workbook, we urge you to provide some comments. Please comment on anything positive, e.g. "What did you like about it?" Also comment on what you did not like. If you have any suggestions, we would also like to hear them. **Congratulations for all your hard work!**

Comments: _____

_____

_____

_____

_____

_____

_____

©2003 Jan Stewart and Hunter House, Inc.

Printed in the USA
CPSIA information can be obtained
at www.ICGtesting.com
JSHW051957150824
68134JS00051B/110

9 781630 2683